Savannah

D0354934

Schiffer
Publishing Ltd

4880 Lower Valley Road Atglen, Pennsylvania 19310

Dedication
For James and Linda Stalcup

Other Schiffer Books on Related Subjects
Art in Savannah: A Guide to the Monuments, Museums, Galleries, and Other Places. Sandra L. Underwood.
The "Bird Girl": The Story of a Sculpture by Sylvia Shaw Judson. Sandra L. Underwood.
Civil War Walking Tour of Savannah. David D'Arcy & Ben Mammina.
Greetings from Savannah. Tina Skinner, Mary Martin, & Nathaniel Wolfgang-Price.
Historic Savannah Postcards. Tina Skinner.
Savannah Ghosts: Haunts of the Hostess City. David Harland Rousseau & Julie Collins Rousseau.
Savannah Sampler Cookbook. Margaret Wayt DeBolt
Savannah Spectres. Margaret Wayt DeBolt.
Savannah Squares: A Keepsake Tour of Gardens, Architecture, and Monuments. Rob Hill.
Savannah Tavern and Pub Reviews. David Rousseau & Dow Harris.
Savannah's Ghosts. Al Cobb.
Savannah's Ghosts II. Al Cobb.

Copyright © 2008 by Jonathan E. Stalcup
Library of Congress Control Number: 2007940473

Designed by John P. Cheek
Cover design by Bruce Waters
Type set in Bernhard Modern BT/Arrus BT

ISBN: 978-0-7643-2907-4
Printed in China

Schiffer Books are available at special discounts for bulk purchases for sales promotions or premiums. Special editions, including personalized covers, corporate imprints, and excerpts can be created in large quantities for special needs. For more information contact the publisher:

Published by Schiffer Publishing Ltd.
4880 Lower Valley Road
Atglen, PA 19310
Phone: (610) 593-1777; Fax: (610) 593-2002
E-mail: Info@schifferbooks.com

For the largest selection of fine reference books on this and related subjects, please visit our web site at **www.schifferbooks.com**
We are always looking for people to write books on new and related subjects. If you have an idea for a book please contact us at the above address.

This book may be purchased from the publisher.
Include $3.95 for shipping.
Please try your bookstore first.
You may write for a free catalog.

In Europe, Schiffer books are distributed by
Bushwood Books
6 Marksbury Ave.
Kew Gardens
Surrey TW9 4JF England
Phone: 44 (0) 20 8392-8585; Fax: 44 (0) 20 8392-9876
E-mail: info@bushwoodbooks.co.uk
Website: www.bushwoodbooks.co.uk
Free postage in the U.K., Europe; air mail at cost.

Contents

Introduction

Before walking around Savannah, it is important to understand the city's layout. The colony's founder, James Edward Oglethorpe, developed Savannah's urban plan as a system of squares and wards. The principles behind it were both utopian and militaristic. The military component was necessary because one of Savannah's main purposes was to extend English occupation further south and keep Spanish Florida from encroaching. Oglethorpe used the Renaissance idea of placing an encampment around a central gathering space or square as his basic cellular unit and then added more cells or wards as the city expanded.

Oglethorpe's utopian idealism came from a desire to offer a better life to Londoners in need of a fresh start. This is still apparent with the separation of public and private buildings around some of Savannah's squares. Each ward was anchored by a square and contained four trust lots and four tything lots. The trust lots faced the square from the east and west sides and were intended for public or civic buildings. Houses were contained in the tything lots on the north and south of each square. Along with certain bans and duties applied to the colonists, the enforcement of public and private buildings in their assigned lots was quickly abandoned. However, the trust lots still bear an air of prominence due to their direct facing of the square and individual use characteristic.

Opposite page:
Map of Savannah's Historic Landmark and Victorian Districts.

Bay Street

Martin Luther King Jr BLVD

East Broad Street

Oglethorpe Avenue

Colonial Park Cemetery

Liberty Street

Gaston Street

Forsyth Park

Park Avenue

Tour Route 1 ———

Tour Route 2 ———

Tour Route 3 ———

Trust Lot

Tything & Other Lots

Start & End Location ✳

While you are walking around Savannah, building locations will be referred to in their respective tything or trust lots so it will be useful to look back at the diagram until you are oriented. The following walks can be completed in less than a couple hours each, but you can also spend a whole day with one walk if you stop into a few of the locations along the way.

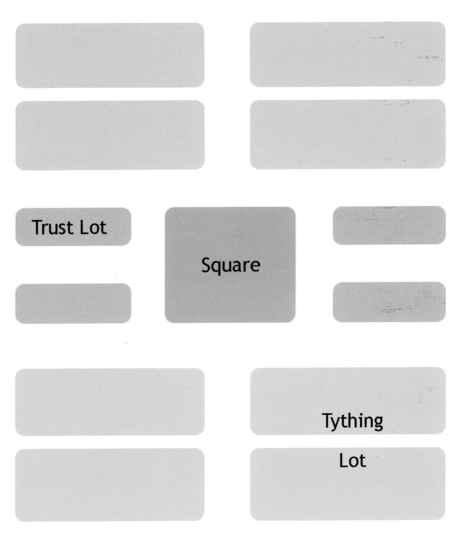

Typical Savannah ward.

Chapter One
Oldest Streets

As Savannah's population expanded, city planners continued to add more squares until the total came to twenty-four squares. This tour will take you through ten of the twelve squares laid out prior to the War of 1812. Few buildings remain from the era before 1812 and the ones that do are mixed with buildings from many other periods in this section of town closest to the river.

Finding a parking space in Savannah's densest neighborhood is difficult and short term. One of the less attractive features of Savannah is its abundance of parking garages. Make these facilities work in your favor by parking on top of them and getting an aerial view of the city. The bottom floor of the Bryan Street Parking Garage is also headquarters for parking services so you can stop in and get a visitor's street pass if you are going to be here for a few days.

As you are walking from the parking garage into Reynolds Square, you will come to a building that was one of the largest in the city when it was built. Now it is one of the smallest buildings facing this square. Although all of the land on this tour was developed prior to the War of 1812, none of the first buildings remain and few structures earlier than 1790 have survived. One notable exception, James Habersham Jr.'s house from 1789, is now known as the Olde Pink House.

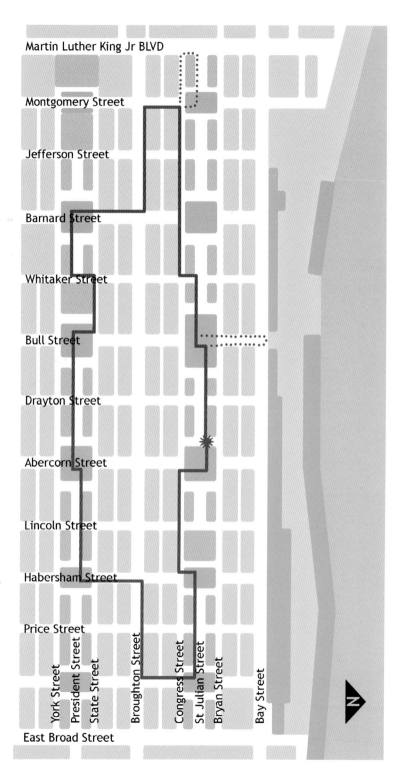

Map showing "Oldest Streets" tour with alternative extensions.

Martin Luther King Jr BLVD

Montgomery Street

Jefferson Street

Barnard Street

Whitaker Street

Bull Street

Drayton Street

Abercorn Street

Lincoln Street

Habersham Street

Price Street

York Street

President Street

State Street

Broughton Street

Congress Street

St Julian Street

Bryan Street

Bay Street

East Broad Street

N

As you are standing in front of Habersham's home, visualize the building without the small wing to the right. Without the addition, you are looking at a "5, 4 & a door." This description refers to the row of five windows on the upper level and the openings directly below them, the middle being a door. This composition is very common in Georgian architecture and the Pink House is Savannah's prime example of the style. Characteristics to look for which make this structure Georgian include the dental molding under the eave, quoins down the corner, and the Palladian window above the porch. The porch itself was added after the War of 1812 when Greek Revival was becoming America's dominant style. This shift in style reflects America pushing away from its mother country, England, and looking to its democratic predecessor, ancient Greece. The next big shift in America's thinking can also be seen on this same house when you look above the windows. The ornamental moldings or dripstones were added after the Civil War when America had become disillusioned with the perfection of democracy and was indulging in the fantasy styles that make up the Victorian era.

James Habersham Jr. House, now the Pink House Restaurant.

Back to back with the Pink House stands the Realty Building. Built in 1924, this building reveals the main theme of early skyscraper design. Inspired by the firm of Adler & Sullivan in Chicago, architects were viewing their new creations like classical Roman columns. The three main parts of a column are the base, shaft, and capital. The capital is where you find the most ornamentation and therefore the earliest skyscrapers tend to have more ornamentation at the top. Although the Realty Building has more ornamentation at the bottom, it still has the tripartite division of heavy base, plain shaft, and dominant capital.

Realty Building.

Look down Drayton Street towards the river before continuing your walk. The building that terminates Drayton Street on the north end is the Cotton Exchange. William Gibbons Preston began his career in Savannah by designing this red brick building after winning the competition sponsored by the Savannah Chamber of Commerce. The date, 1886, is woven into the terracotta design at the top of the building. More terracotta covers the rest of the façade, which in turn is supported on iron columns that allow Drayton Street to continue underneath the Cotton Exchange to the river.

The style used for the Cotton Exchange is Romanesque Revival. The man given the most credit for popularizing a revival of the medieval Romanesque style is Henry Hobson Richardson. Richardson was raised in New Orleans and studied at Harvard, and later the Ecole de Beaux Art in Paris. After absorbing more information about medieval European architecture than he was taught in school, Richardson returned to Boston and began designing a hybrid style. Although many traits characterize a Richardsonian Romanesque building, the most important is a monumental arch similar to the one above the entry of the Cotton Exchange.

Cotton Exchange.

To the northeast of the Realty Building is Citizens Bank, designed by Gottfried Norman. Completed in 1895, the Citizens Bank building has more detail at the top than the Realty Building. Notice the use of rough hewn stone at the base of the building and the intricately carved stone in various places, including the porthole dotted frieze at the top. The top row of arched windows is similar to windows used by Louis Sullivan, who was in turn inspired by H.H. Richardson.

Citizens Bank, now occupied by the Savannah College of Art and Design.

Directly across Drayton Street from the Realty Building, you will see Bank of America. Designed as Citizens and Southern National Bank by Mowbray and Uffinger, this New York firm also designed the 1911, fifteen story Savannah Bank and Trust Company building on the corner of Bryan and Bull Streets. Notice the top of this building is like a classical temple elevated above the pedestrians into the clouds. The only other building close to its height today is the Forest City Hotel Company Building directly to the south. Three notable skyscrapers once continued the lofty dialogue in the southeast tything but were removed to make room for the red brick Suntrust complex in the 1970s.

Savannah Bank and Trust Company Building.

Because most of the buildings surrounding Johnson Square are banks, it is known as "Bank Square." The notable exception is Christ Church on the southwest trust lot. Built in 1838, this Greek Revival structure sits on the same piece of land intended for Oglethorpe's Anglican congregation in 1733. As the oldest congregation in Savannah, it seems fitting to find them in such a stately and serious structure. Originally, meetings were held in a small wooden shed. Local planter, James Hamilton Couper, designed the shell of the current building after graduating from Yale and spending time in Europe. Couper is best described as a gentleman architect and his building has characteristics that seem more Roman than Greek. One major detail that has been altered from Couper's original design is the staircase leading to the portico. Once a straight stair the width of the building, it led directly from the street to door.

Christ Church.

Stand in Johnson Square and look towards the north to see the gold dome of City Hall. Completed in 1906 by Hyman Witcover, the dome has only been gold since 1987 when a private donation was made to the city to pay for gold leaf to be applied. Before being gold leafed, the crowning element on this neoclassical building was copper, eventually painted green to look like the patina underneath. Although most domes referenced those on churches in Europe, they became an important feature on many government buildings after the Capitol in Washington D.C. was crowned with a dome in the 1860s.

City Hall.

To make room for City Hall's construction, the City Exchange had to be demolished. A replica of the 1799 exchange building's bell tower sits on the ground in the park to the east of the current City Hall. After growing up in France and living in New York and Savannah, Adrien Boucher designed the City Exchange in a blocky, symmetrical mass with classical influences. The gothic tower, rising from a more classical inspired building, must be an example of what Boucher proposed to teach when he offered architectural drawing classes in Savannah in 1802.

Replica of City Exchange cupola.

Across Bay Street from City Hall is the United States Custom House. The federal government has maintained a building in Savannah in the form of a customs house since the 1790s; however, the current building was completed in 1852. The Federal government, instead of the local citizens, made the choice for the architect of this important building. Savannahians made an effort to have resident architect Charles Blaney Cluskey appointed to design the new structure, but the commission went to New York architect John S. Norris. The new, Northern architect brought granite down from the North to build with but used local labor. He was soon in favor with the city and received many more commissions for both public buildings and private residences until he moved back to New York at the beginning of the Civil War.

The most dominant feature of the Greek Revival Custom House is its front portico. Composed of six columns, the porch does not follow any of the three major Greek classical orders but is instead influenced by the Tower of the Winds in Athens. Rather than stacking rings of granite, the columns were each formed as a single unit. Accounts hold that the weight involved required them to be slowly hoisted up the bluff from the river over a thirty-day period, and getting the columns up the steep steps and into place on the porch took another thirty days. The lack of bases on these columns is archeologically correct, and adds to the sublime sense of power being conveyed by the entire building. Even the stairs convey a sense of power, with the bottom steps pushing past the fence onto the sidewalk and into the flow of foot traffic in front of the building.

United States Custom House.

River Street, Factors Walk, and ramp to Bay Street.

Standing near the Custom House and City Hall on Bay Street will give you an opportunity to understand the architecture of Bay Street, Factors Walk, and River Street. This strip of land along the river bluff is tied to Savannah's early shipping economy and started being developed in the current manner in the 1790s. Cotton was the most important product being shipped from Savannah. The men who benefited directly from the crop were cotton factors. Factors Walk is the street halfway down the bluff running parallel with Bay Street at the top and River Street at the bottom of the bluff. Factors began their day crossing bridges from Bay Street to their offices. As they entered their offices, they were able to look down onto Factors Walk and see what shipments were coming into the middle section of their warehouses. Finally the cotton reached the lower level and went out to the ships on the river.

If you walked to the river, go back to Johnson Square and turn to the west to pass two more banks. The postmodern Palmer & Cay building on the northwest trust lot lends a remark from the 1980s with its strong lines and recessed lower level giving the entrance a feeling of power and importance. In the southeast trust lot the Coastal Bank, built as Chatham Bank in 1912, resembles a vault and lets you know your money is safe behind its solid walls. The crypt-like quality of the Chatham Bank relates effectively with the William Strickland-designed Nathanael Greene monument in the center of the square that takes its obelisk form from Egyptian funerary structures. Chatham Bank, now Coastal Bank.

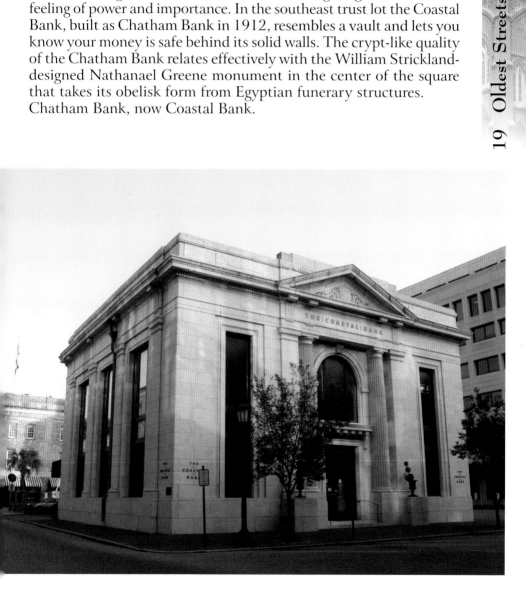

Chatham Bank, now Coastal Bank.

Leaving the banks behind and heading to Ellis Square, you may notice a line of people waiting to get into Lady and Sons on the west side of Whitaker Street. This restaurant is housed in the Thomas Gibbons block. Gibbons' father warned the son to build a strong building that would last forever. Considering the many fire hazards and redevelopment plans in this area, the late Georgian structure can be considered a strong survivor in spite of its extreme wear. To get an idea of the original appearance, first notice the quoins, or corner blocks, laid in alternating directions. Next count over three windows on the longer façade or two windows on the shorter and observe a worn pilaster or attached column, most of which still have their bases but are missing the original fluting and heavy Corinthian capitals that were placed just below the cornice. The main details placing this 1820 building into its Greek Revival time period are the lintels which once had an abstracted Greek Key motif carved into their soft sandstone.

Continuing past the Gibbons Block, you will come to Ellis Square. One of the first four squares, Ellis Square was originally Market Square and served as the gathering space for vendors. A series of market structures were placed on the square and the last was a grand warehouse type demolished in 1954 to make room for a parking garage. Although several grand buildings were lost in Savannah, this is the one that ignited citizens enough to form the Historic Savannah Foundation and caused hundreds of other buildings to be saved. By placing a fifty year lease on the subsequent parking garage, citizens were given enough time to reach the conclusion that the area should fall back into the rhythm of the squares and, with changes in technology, a parking garage could be completely submerged in the sand, greatly increasing capacity from the former parking structure.

Thomas Gibbons Block with Lady & Sons in east end.

Germania Fire Company Building, now Garibaldi Restaurant.

You will see attractive storefronts and warehouse buildings that functioned as part of the market area as you continue west towards Franklin Square on Congress Street. On the left side of the street you will come upon the Germania Fire Company building from 1871. Notice the arched windows on the second floor, including a central Palladian window. Behind all these arches lies a neoclassical ballroom that indicates how good business was for the fire company.

On the right side of Congress, just before entering the square, you will pass Belford's restaurant in a building originally built for the Hebrew Congregation in 1902 and possibly designed by Hyman Witcover. The Belford family purchased the building from the Hebrew Congregation in 1913, and it became a wholesale food store, one of many such buildings in the market district.

Hebrew Congregation building, now Belford's Restaurant.

Taking a long view down Congress, you can see the yellow stucco on the Scarborough House across Martin Luther King Junior Boulevard. If you have extra time, you might want to explore this building further, but come back to Franklin Square to continue the tour. Designed in the Classical Revival style by William Jay, William and Julia Scarborough's home served as a school from 1878 until 1962 and then fell into ruin

Scarborough House, now the Ships of the Sea – Maritime Museum.

until the current owner, the Ships of the Sea – Maritime Museum, acquired the property. Although Adrien Boucher designed the 1799 City Exchange and offered architectural drawing classes in Savannah in 1802, nothing attributable to him remains and Jay is generally considered the city's first trained architect. The Scarborough House is one of three documented Jay homes that remain in Savannah.

Perhaps the most significant building on Franklin Square is the First African Baptist Church. Although the congregation dates from the 1770s, the current building dates from 1861. The projecting middle bay forming the steeple on the front façade was added in the 1870s and was originally much taller. More information about the building and congregation is available in the church's museum.

First African Baptist Church.

As you turn to the south to walk down Montgomery Street, take a minute to gaze down the street and realize there used to be two more squares interrupting the view. Elbert, Liberty, and Franklin Squares were all cut through when I-16 finished onto Montgomery Street in 1960. Only Franklin Square has been reassembled and Elbert and Liberty are now referred to as the Lost Squares.

View of Montgomery Street from Broughton Street.

Walk down Montgomery Street and turn left onto Broughton Street. Broughton is undergoing renewal and you will see many shops. If you have the time, stop in and support the local economy. Architecturally, Broughton Street exhibits a variety of storefront design from the 1850s Greek Revival to more recent Art Deco.

View of Broughton Street from Montgomery Street.

At the intersection of Broughton and Barnard Streets, you will notice two Art Deco buildings whose current use is labeled underneath the historic signs from the previous owners. On the northeast corner is the Kress building from 1923. Now broken into lofts on the top two stories and occupied by Gap on the main floor and Jazz'd Tapas Bar in the basement, the building you see today is twice the size of the original. In 1938 the five-and-dime was extended on the Broughton Street side from three bays to the current six.

Kress Building, now the Gap.

Opposite the Kress building, on the southwest corner of the same intersection, is the Weed Building. From 1904, the building operated as Silver's Five-and-Dime. The restored gold lettered signage on red background that wraps around the building between the first and second floors today makes it appear that this is the current use; however, if you look below this sign to the fringe of the awning, you can see that it is now Clipper Trading Company. On top of the building there was once a sign standing approximately twenty feet off the building reading "Silver's, 5 & 10¢ store, nothing over $1.00" that would light up at night.

Weed Building/Silver's Five-and-Dime, now the Clipper Trading Company.

Walk down Barnard Street towards the south from Broughton Street. The square in front of you was originally St. James Square, but was renamed Telfair Square in honor of the family whose home you will see to the right in the northeast trust lot of the square. Built for Alexander Telfair in 1820, this is another home designed by William Jay. Notice the semicircular or Diocletian window above the entry. This is the same type Jay used on the Scarborough house although the columns here are Corinthian instead of Doric. When you look at the side of the building, notice there are three sections to the structure. The middle portion rises slightly higher than the front or back and occupies the area previously containing the courtyard. This portion was built in the 1880s after Alexander Telfair's sister, Mary Telfair, willed the house to become an art museum. The architect in charge of the expansion was Danish born Detlef Lienau, one of the founding members of the American Institute of Architects.

Telfair Mansion, now the Telfair Academy of Arts and Sciences.

The Telfair Museum of Art is housed in three buildings today. The mansion you've just observed, The Owens-Thomas house you will see shortly, and the Jepson Center visible on the southeast tything lot, on the other side of Trinity Methodist Church from the Telfair Academy. As you walk to the Jepson Center, you may be drawn into the Methodist church by organ music coming out the open door. If you do go in, notice how the wall facing the entry of this 1848 Greek Revival building designed by John Hogg echoes the front façade with columns and a triangular pediment.

Trinity Methodist Church.

The Jepson Center, designed by Moshe Safdie, was completed in March of 2006. The large sheets of glass used for the façade open a visual dialogue between the lobby and the square and invite people to become part of the art being displayed. The large site-cast concrete frames holding the glass in place also act as columns and help define the street wall that is important for the community room created in the square. The overall design of the building is a subtractive sculpture with spaces that feel as though they have been scooped out of a masonry block. Standing in the green square, you can look up the grand staircase that slices diagonally through the building and at the top of the stair, you can see the top of the trees on the far side of the building. Walk to the Barnard Street side of the building and note how the lane is preserved and the sculpture terraces sit on shorter masses, evoking the typical Savannah rhythm of carriage houses facing a lane with their higher townhouses facing away towards main streets. Another rhythm taken from local townhouses is a fenestration that includes long lower windows with shorter windows above. This is seen with the openings to the museum store on the ground floor and the café above it.

Jepson Center for the Arts.

To the east of the Jepson Center, you will see the federal government office complex referred to by the local population as "the bathroom tile buildings." These postmodern structures were finished in the 1980s with several references to historic architecture. On the Barnard Street side of the larger building, notice the massing is broken up like a row of townhouses. The lane has not been preserved, but a reference is made to it with the entry to the underground parking occurring in its place. On the two smaller buildings, there are front porches, with columns, that look across the square at their Greek revival counterparts. The tops of the postmodern porches have streamlining that mimics the curves from Art Moderne buildings. All three buildings in this complex have banded rustication in the granite base, a parapet wall delineated with a granite band course, and fenestration that is broken up rather than a solid glass curtain wall.

Federal Government office complex.

Take a moment to observe a small building on the corner of Whitaker and State Streets to the north of the tile buildings. This unassuming structure bears an important silver plaque on its south façade. It is a LEED certificate award. LEED stands for Leadership in Energy and Environmental Design, a rating system used as a set of guidelines by designers. The developer leading the movement in Savannah with this project is Melavor Inc., and for this design, they teamed up with Dawson Wissmach Architects. A LEED building is also referred to as Sustainable and reuse of materials is one of the best ways to sustain the environment. In this case, the most obvious material being reused is the shell of the building. The roof is something that was replaced and by doing so the team was able to greatly improve the insulation of the building and, therefore, use less energy to heat and cool it.

Melavor's Whitaker Street building with LEED silver certificate.

On the other side of Whitaker you will see the marble clad Federal Courthouse designed by Jeremiah O'Rourke in the 1890s and added to in the 1930s with William Aiken acting as supervisory architect. When first completed, the building was contained in the south trust lot of Wright Square. The current composition extends across President Street into the north trust lot as well. Although eclectic, the dominant style of the building is Romanesque Revival with Renaissance Revival heavily influencing the addition. If you're looking at the building from Wright Square, you may be able to see a small portion of the tower above the roof, but it you look at it from Whitaker Street, you can see much more of the tower. The base of the tower was originally a main entry to the building and helps you to understand how much the building has expanded.

Federal Courthouse from Whitaker Street.

Federal Courthouse
from Wright Square.

The main theme in the buildings around Wright Square is Romanesque Revival. Directly across the square from the original section of the Federal Courthouse, you will see the yellow bricks on the old County Courthouse. This is another design by W. G. Preston. In his original design for the courthouse, Preston included lots of rough hewn stone over arches, the building was a story shorter and there was a large entry on the longer façade facing President Street. In the final design, he was forced to economize. Look at the windows on the third floor facing the square and notice that they are rectangular windows placed behind brick arches. Preston has managed to keep some important elements like the battered granite foundation which angles towards the building like the base of a castle. He also has several small, corbelled turrets that look like copper capped bullets around the top edge of the building.

Old Chatham
County Courthouse.

In the trust lot north of the old County Courthouse sits the Lutheran Church of the Ascension. This building also has large Roman arches and replaces an older Greek Revival structure. Although George B. Clarke finished the current structure in 1879, the congregation dates from 1741, making it one of the oldest congregations in Georgia. The sanctuary is often open so you may want to take a few minutes to see its large barrel vault and brass pulpit. To get to this space, you have to climb several stairs. Instead of a large external staircase like the Christ Church entry, this has been internalized. Both churches raise themselves away from the street to prevent dust and noise from coming through windows that would need to be opened in the hot summer.

Lutheran Church of the Ascension.

Before leaving Wright Square, notice one more Romanesque Revival building in the southeast tything lot. This red brick structure was designed by Alfred Eichberg and finished in 1890 for John Schwarz. In this case, a metal frame is holding up the floors and the brick is hanging off the structure in the form of a curtain wall like the skyscrapers in Johnson Square. It also seems convenient to have the German Lutheran church in close proximity. The architect, Eichberg, was born in New York, raised in Atlanta, and trained in Heidelberg, Germany. This building was the closest he came to designing a skyscraper in Savannah and even has a curved corner that predates most flatiron buildings.

John Schwarz building, now Wachovia Bank.

Exit Wright Square to the east and continue towards Oglethorpe Square. On the way you will see more arches on the Standard Oil Company Building on the corner of Drayton and President. This early filling station was rehabilitated into a drive through bank in the space where there were once gas pumps.

Standard Oil Company, now Sea Island Bank.

Across President Street from the Standard Oil Company Building, a parking lot is located where there used to be three townhouses built for Mary Marshall. The double houses facing Oglethorpe Square were part of the project and give you an idea of what the missing houses looked like. Altogether, these houses show the important role of female developers in nineteenth century Savannah. Mary Marshall had several properties around Savannah and the ones remaining include a row of four on Oglethorpe Avenue and Marshall House Hotel on Broughton Street. All of her remaining properties are from the 1850s, making them antebellum and pre paved streets. Because the streets were sand until the 1870s, most houses and churches had their main level raised off the street. The double houses you are looking at in Oglethorpe Square's southwest trust lot internalized the front stair that you find on the outside of most homes prior to the 1870s.

Double houses built for Mary Marshall.

In the southwest tything lot you will see the old Marine Hospital from 1907, recently rehabilitated into administrative offices for Savannah College of Art and Design. This building exhibits the Spanish Colonial Revival style seldom seen in Savannah. Rough stucco, unornamented arches, and terracotta tile roofing all add to the building's distinctive look.

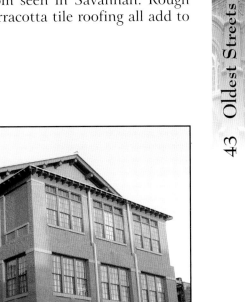

Marine Hospital, now occupied by the Savannah College of Art and Design.

Another building with unornamented arches is the Owens-Thomas house in the northeast trust lot. These arches come from classical architecture and frame windows on another house designed by William Jay. Notice how the front porch of this house is similarly proportioned to the Telfair and Scarborough homes, but the columns are Ionic where the other two were Doric and Corinthian. Although all three homes are from the English Regency, Jay is showing some of the diversity from that period. Instead of a Diocletian window, this house has a large niche housing its entry. Along with the bowed colonnade, the niche implies a circle in plan. Newly discovered Roman villas strongly influenced Classical Revival architecture and several shaped rooms are included in this design. Jay grew up in Bath, England, and apprenticed with D. R. Roper in London where at an early age he exhibited several designs at the Royal Academy.

The Owens-Thomas house was Jay's first major commission and was built for his relative through marriage, Richard Richardson. Richardson married into an established Savannah family and this house made a statement about his newly achieved status. Unfortunately he wasn't able to hold onto this status when a fire struck the city in 1820, a year after the house was completed. The fire destroyed 60-70% of the city and was followed by a yellow fever epidemic that killed approximately 700 people. Due to the fever outbreak, the port was

Owens-Thomas House.

quarantined and with a national financial panic already underway, the Savannah economy was hit hard. Although Richardson and Jay both left town, their house survived and influenced local architecture. Even in the most contemporary buildings, similarities can be found with this house. Notice the banded rustication on the foundation, like the federal tile buildings on Telfair Square. Also on Telfair Square is the Jepson Center with an interior bridge unremarkable for contemporary architecture but similar to one in the Owens-Thomas house unique for its time.

One of the most direct influences on Savannah architecture was the use of cast iron. The Grecian balcony on the south side of the Owens-Thomas house was the largest use of cast iron in the city, if not the country, when Jay brought it from England. Once it was here, Jay started working with Henry McAlpin to produce iron at the Hermitage Plantation north of town where McAlpin also produced Savannah gray bricks. A painting of McAlpin, along with more iron and other technological innovations are found within the Owens-Thomas house and you can stop here for a tour to see them. As you continue to the carriage house and slave quarters at the back of the house, you will see a missing section of stucco on the garden wall that gives you an idea of how the house is constructed. The material under the stucco is tabby, a concrete that uses oyster shells. This material was probably chosen by builder John Retan in order to support the weight of an indoor plumbing system that included large cisterns in the upper floors.

Tabby construction found under stucco of the Owens-Thomas House.

When leaving the Owens Thomas house, cross Lincoln Street and walk towards Columbia Square. Facing the square in the northwest trust lot is the Kehoe house. Built in 1893, William Kehoe moved into this massive Queen Anne house from the ivy-covered 1885 Italianate town house located diagonally across the square. By the late 1800s, there were several sources of iron in Savannah and Kehoe was in charge of one of the largest. He came to America as the son of poor Irish immigrants and worked his way up in the iron industry to head his own company in 1883. Kehoe's home is also his three-dimensional catalogue with the moldings above the first floor windows differing from the second, and the columns on the front differing from the side porch. All of these details, along with the railings, brackets, and interior ceiling medallions, advertised what you could buy from the Kehoe foundry. Kehoe's architect, Dewitt Bruyn, added his client's product to imported brick and terracotta to form an eclectic creation larger than any other house in this ward.

Queen Anne house built for William Kehoe.

Of more moderate proportions than the Kehoe house is the 1820 Davenport House on the northwest tything lot. This was the first building Historic Savannah Foundation saved after they formed in the wake of City Market being demolished in 1954. The home they saved is Savannah's premiere example of Federal era architecture. Thomas Jefferson started the architecture of this time by using parts of Classical architecture along with lots of exposed red brick and white trim. Isaiah Davenport was a master builder or carpenter, rather than a trained architect. Like many others in Savannah, he brought his knowledge to Savannah from the northeast states. For his private residence, Davenport constructed a "5, 4 & a door" similar to the Georgian style Pink House, but unlike James Habersham's home, this has a service area at ground level and the main floor is raised above the sand street. The double curved steps that rise up to the front stoop are similar to the entry steps William Jay designed for the Owens-Thomas house and are possibly the first influence seen in Savannah from the young English architect. Like Kehoe, Davenport was designing a house he could use as an advertisement and included features other people in Savannah might want on their new homes. An element typical of the Federal era is the entry with its elliptical fanlight drawn out on top of the sidelights.

Davenport House.

Leave the Davenport House and walk down Habersham Street to the north to return to Broughton Street. At the intersection of Habersham and Broughton Streets, you will have a good opportunity to understand the evolution of Broughton from mainly residential to mainly commercial. The blue house at 401 East Broughton Street was built in 1822 for Humphrey Gwathney and was one of many such clapboard-sided, raised stoop homes on Broughton Street. After several fires, changing glass technology, and production of cast iron storefronts, what was once a residential street has become primarily commercial. Before they were completely demolished, many homes were raised a few extra feet into the air so a new storefront could be fitted underneath. An example of this is John Berrien's house located diagonally from Gwathney's. Berrien's house was completed in the 1790s as a "5, 4 & a door" on a raised basement like the Davenport house. In 1917, the Berrien house was raised a couple extra feet to its current height and the storefront was applied to the bottom portion. Originally it would have been closer to the height of the Gwathney house that is back to its original height and single-family use after a century's use as a store.

Humphrey Gwathney House.

Walk down Broughton and turn left onto Houston Street to get to Washington Square. At the corner of Broughton and Houston is the 1884 house built for John Rourke. This is a useful comparison to Kehoe's first house as it is a year earlier and Rourke also owned a large iron foundry in Savannah. Both homes exhibit Italianate characteristics with their bracketed eves and segmental arched windows.

John Rourke House.

Italianate house built for William Kehoe.

Surrounding Washington Square are many homes and a large cotton warehouse complex built for George Boifeuillet in 1860 that now houses the Mulberry Inn. The imposing masonry structure was well suited to its use as a Coca-Cola bottling plant in the early 1900s and its current name looks back at one of the earliest unrealized hopes for the area—a silk producing colony. It is fitting that it sits in the vicinity of the original Trustees Garden, set up as the first experimental garden when the colonist arrived from England in 1733. It was the hope of the king and trustees that Savannah would produce a number of agriculture exports and although they documented producing eight pounds of silk, the industry never succeeded.

George Boifeuillet Warehouse, now the Mulberry Inn.

Notice the shells imbedded in the concrete supports of the park benches and the concrete end table blocks in the square. The same material can be seen on St. Julian Street between Washington and Warren Squares. While this looks similar to the tabby used in the construction of the Owens-Thomas house, it is more appropriate to call it faux tabby. This is modern concrete from the 1960s, with shells mixed in. It is a unique quoting of a historic material being used for objects and surfaces that would not have been made with tabby in the eighteenth and nineteenth centuries.

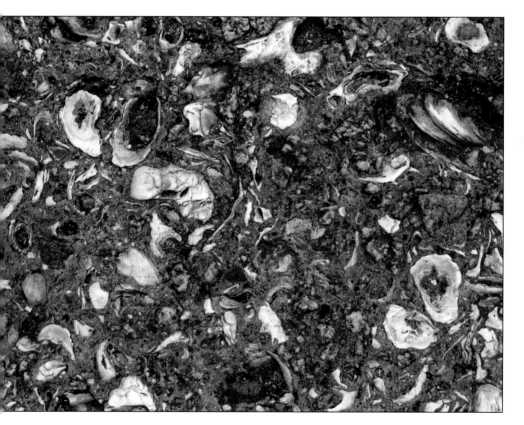

St. Julian Street paved with a simulation of tabby.

Walking along the faux tabby section of St. Julian Street is one of your best opportunities to experience what the city might have actually felt like before the War of 1812, although the street would have been sand and only a few buildings actually predate this early war. On the north side of the street, at 510 East St. Julian, there is a

small cottage built for Revolutionary War Major Charles Oddingsells in 1797. If this home is fairly typical for early Savannah, an anomaly can be found directly across the street with Hampton Lillibridge's house at 507 East St. Julian.

Charles Oddingsells House.

Hampton Lillibridge moved to Savannah from Newport, Rhode Island, and constructed a home in a style more common in the North. The most unique characteristic of the Lillibridge house is its gambrel roof. Instead of a single pitch per side like a standard gable roof, the gambrel roof is pitched twice on each side. This roof type is Dutch in origin and was fairly common in the North but you may be looking at the only surviving Southern example from the eighteenth century. There were originally two gambrel-roofed houses built by Lillibridge in the 1790s. One house collapsed when they were both being moved to the remaining home's current location.

Savannah's famous preservationist, Jim Williams, restored the Lillibridge, Oddingsells, and several other neighboring houses in the 1950s and 1960s. Some, like the Lillibridge house, had to be moved to their current locations before restoration could commence. Another house moved to its current location is the small cottage on the corner of Price Street at 426 East St. Julian built for Henry Willink in 1845 and occupied by Jane Deveaux, a free person of color, who ran a secret school from it prior to the Civil War.

Hampton Lillibridge House.

If you visually delete the front porch, Jane Deveaux's home is very similar to the first cottages set up when Oglethorpe arrived in 1733. The central door with a window on each side echoes the first cottages, but the proportions are different. The early cottages were 24 feet facing the street, 16 feet deep, and 8 feet to the ceiling. The lower level was partitioned into three small rooms, and there was a sleeping loft in the attic. Deveaux's home exhibits another roof type brought down from the Northeast—the saltbox or catslide roof. Generally this roof type is found on homes with a two-story front façade and a one-story rear façade but the shape achieved is the same short pitch at the front and longer pitch at the back found here. The purpose behind this roof type is retention of warmth during harsh northern winters. As with the Willink-Deveaux house, the longer section of the roof faces north and allows the wind from that direction to easily flow over the house. In areas with lots of snow, the snow gathers on the roof and creates an extra layer of insulation, but in Savannah that is a rare occurrence and not worth building for.

Willink-Deveaux House.

Proceed to Warren Square to see homes more typical of Savannah circa 1800. In the northeast trust lot is the George Basil Spencer house and in the southeast trust lot, the John David Mongin house. Notice that both homes follow the "5, 4 & a door" layout, although the windows on the Spencer house are smaller than the windows on the Mongin house. The entry porch and stairs to the Mongin house were added when the home was moved from across the square in the 1960s. During the move, the house was also lowered off its original raised basement. When you look at the chimneys, you see three flues indicating three fireplaces on each end of the house. One fireplace would have been at each end of the missing lower level. The Spencer house is less typical with its chimneys at the rear; most Southern homes of the period had their chimneys on the end while Northern homes from the same time put the chimney in the center, allowing heat to radiate through the entire house. The Southern response to a hot climate was to only build the houses one room deep, allowing cross ventilation. Most homes lost this wind benefit as families grew and additions were made to the back of the houses.

John David Mongin House.

Look around Warren Square to see other examples of vernacular Georgian homes. On the north side of the square there are two more clapboard sided structures. The orange building with two doors at the corner of Habersham and Bryan Streets was originally a "5, 4 & a door" when it was built in 1809, but windows were shifted and another door and hall added to make it double houses in the 1890s.

There is also a large parking garage facing Warren Square that violates Oglethorpe's plan by sitting on St. Julian Street in order to connect two trust lots and create more parking. By going around the parking garage to get back to Reynolds Square, the scenery should start to look familiar, if you began the tour here. The James Habersham Jr. House should look even more impressive after seeing that most large houses at the time were like the Mongin and Spencer houses in the last square. Take a few more minutes to observe this pre-1812 structure and consider how much American history is told with one pink house.

Dr. William Parker House.

Chapter Two
Growing City

Savannah had a large growth spurt starting in 1793 with the invention of the cotton gin on nearby Mulberry Grove plantation. Before the cotton gin, there was some production of cotton, but more important was rice production. Both were labor intensive, and rice required lots of standing water. Standing water led to mosquitoes and yellow fever, and although the colonists didn't understand the mosquito link, they did know there was some connection between rice paddies and yellow fever.

Cotton became even more preferable to rice when there was a machine to speed up the seed removal or ginning. The population of enslaved people grew, so more cotton could come out of the field to be ginned. In town, enslaved and free persons of color became part of the local building culture. Merchants, laborers, artisans, and other professionals from across the racial spectrum made a living connected to the cotton planters and factors and added to the diversity of Savannah's architecture.

Cotton continued to be the economic stabilizer after the Civil War. Although the land was being worn out by planting the same crop on it every year, the downfall of cotton in America was the introduction of the boll weevil. The small pest wiped out Georgia's crop by 1920 and signaled the end of the cotton era. The financial backing required for new architecture slowed dramatically from the 1920s until the 1960s in Savannah. The economy began to pick up again in the 1960s with tourism, the ports, and the beginning of Savannah College of Art and Design at the end of the 1970s. By this time, Savannah's preservation movement was well under way and new architecture had to coexist with a large percentage of nineteenth century survivors.

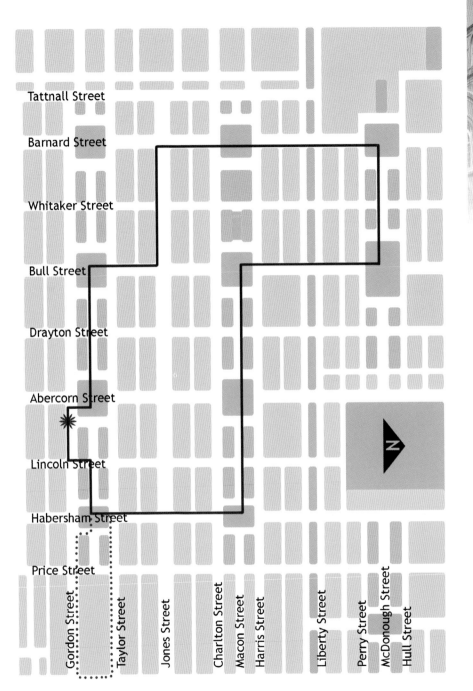

Tattnall Street

Barnard Street

Whitaker Street

Bull Street

Drayton Street

Abercorn Street

Lincoln Street

Habersham Street

Price Street

Gordon Street

Taylor Street

Jones Street

Charlton Street

Macon Street

Harris Street

Liberty Street

Perry Street

McDonough Street

Hull Street

Map showing "Growing City" tour with alternative extensions.

A great starting point for this tour is Massie Heritage Center on Calhoun Square. There is plenty of free parking in the neighborhood and there are several bed and breakfast locations nearby. There are a few great displays in this historic school about historic preservation, architectural styles, and the development of Savannah's urban plan. Part of the building they are housed in was built as Savannah's first public school in 1856. The middle section is John Norris' original design and wings were added in 1872 and 1886 that replicate the original Greek Revival building.

Massie Heritage Center.

The triangular pediment capping the Massie School is repeated above the windows of the townhouses directly across the square. Also characteristic of a Greek Revival townhouse are the large windows and dentil molding at the top of the building. Look around the square to find more variations of townhouses with both Greek Revival and Italianate features. Aside from the details being slightly different, most of the homes on this square are three stories with an attic. From the ground up, the floors are divided into service, public, and private. In many homes of the period, the service areas, such as the kitchen and laundry, were relegated to an outbuilding. In Savannah, the lot sizes were relatively small so the service area was placed under the houses. The streets were all sand and traffic created a cloud of dust that was better avoided by placing the public level on the second story referred to as the piano nobile, or locally, as the parlor floor. The least used areas of a townhouse are the top floors. These private levels contain sleeping and storage rooms, areas that do not need to be accessed as often. Placing sleeping at the top of a house also allows Savannahians to capture cooler breezes in the hot summer months.

Houses built by and for George Ash.

Along with all the houses around Calhoun Square, there is a church. Wesley Monumental United Methodist Church is sited on the southwest trust lot. This 1876-90 High Victorian Gothic structure designed by Dixon and Carson is named for the founder of Methodism, John Wesley. Wesley is important to Savannah's history because he came from England in 1735 as the city's Anglican preacher. Although John Wesley and his brother Charles only stayed in Savannah for a short time, a Methodist congregation was named for them in 1807. After several congregational moves, the current structure's exterior was completed in the 1870s. Originally the entry to the church was at ground level before the current staircase was constructed in the 1900s. The towers have also had slight alterations but were always at their dramatically differing heights to give the appearance of being built at different times.

Wesley Monumental
Methodist Church.

The back of the Methodist church faces the back of Mickve Israel Synagogue. Although the congregation dates from 1733, making it the third oldest Jewish congregation in the country, their current temple structure was completed in 1878. Although many synagogues were designed in the Moorish Revival style in the 1800s, a few were following the fashionable Gothic Revival used by Henry Harrison and later, J.D. Foley for Mickve Israel. Defining elements include pointed gothic arches, stained glass windows, buttresses, and a cruciform plan revealing itself on the exterior by pushing the transept bay higher than the side aisle roof. Even the circular clerestory windows are highlighted with the gothic quatrefoil design. Castle architecture also influences this High Victorian Gothic building with a battlement on the entry tower. Notice how the spire adds a Moorish flair to the synagogue with its ogee dome.

Mickve Israel Synagogue.

Anchored by the Pulaski Monument, Monterey Square is surrounded by homes that have earned it much attention. The most famous house on this square is the Mercer-Williams House directly across from Mickve Israel Synagogue. Made famous by the New York Times bestseller, *Midnight in the Garden of Good and Evil*, and the movie of the same title, this landmark is still a private home that serves a dual purpose as a museum. Construction began on the house in 1860 for Hugh Mercer, the great-grandfather of songwriter Johnny Mercer, but no Mercer ever lived in the house after it was finished in 1871. Its most famous occupant was preservationist and antiques dealer, Jim Williams.

House built for Hugh Mercer and restored by Jim Williams.

Noble Hardee House.

The Italianate style Mercer house was designed by New York native John Norris before the Civil War. Norris moved back to New York when the war started. Construction halted on several building projects, including the Noble Hardee house at 3 West Gordon in the southwest tything lot. Both Italianate houses were finished after the war, Mercer house by Norris's former assistant, DeWitt Bruyn. Architects had returned to Roman architecture for inspiration for centuries. However, Italianate was the first style for which architects went back to Italy for design inspiration and looked at domestic architecture rather than the high style Roman architecture. Many Italianate homes are asymmetrical with rooms projecting in various directions, and they often have a tower similar to an authentic Italian farmhouse that evolved through several generations. Instead of being asymmetrical, the Nobel Hardee house and Mercer-Williams house achieve the Italianate style with their details. Both homes have heavy brackets under their eaves and segmental arches. The brackets imply structural roof timbers projecting into view. The segmental arches are flatter than a half-circle Roman arch and the circle implied by the curve goes well outside the window opening. The segmental arches on Mercer house each cover two Roman arches and exhibit the Italianate use of paired sash windows; this was the first style to use such a feature.

Leaving Monterey Square on the north side, you are walking down Bull Street towards the river. Bull Street has always been the important street in town, and, in the early 1800s, started evolving into a monument alley. Today it is zero in the east to west numbering system. In the 1980s, Mills Lane donated funds and research to the city to enable the burial of power lines, recasting of the Shepherd-crook light poles, and installation of barrel-shaped, cast iron trashcans modeled after ones in Paris.

View of Bull Street from Monterey Square.

The first traffic crossing you will come to after leaving Monterey Square is a lane. Notice the modern use of trashcans and utility lines, but also the historic carriage houses. Many of the carriage houses still have larger openings where the carriage entered, and now some cars drive in to use the space as a garage. Sometimes you will spot the outline in the upper floor of a large opening that once received hay into the loft. Servants would have been quartered in parts of the structures and now many carriage houses are rented to students, other downtown residents, and the occasional business.

Like most lanes, the one you are looking down does not have a street sign. In order to know the name of the lane, you have to know the name of the street that parallels it to the north. The next street you will come to is Jones Street, so this is Jones Lane.

Jones Street is one of the most desirable addresses in the city due to its width, age, and large trees. Standing on the corner of Bull and Jones, you are on the older section of Jones, laid out in the 1840s. This was a time when wide streets were not often executed for residential use. When Oglethorpe conceived Savannah's plan, he was not thinking of carriages so much as military use and the wide streets reflect this mindset.

View of Jones Lane from Bull Street.

On the northeast and southwest corners of the Jones and Bull Streets intersection are homes built for Alexander Smets and Israel Tefft, two founders of the Georgia Historical Society, an archival library. It is fitting that Alexander Smets, who lived in the red brick house on the northeast corner, owned the largest collection of rare books in the South. Unfortunately for him, he later had to sell all of them at auction in New York after the Civil War.

Smets' home is attributed to John Norris. Although much simpler than Norris' design for Mercer House, there is a similarity with the refined red brick and large double porch covering the back of the house. On Smets' house, Norris placed the entry at ground level facing a still unpaved street. Instead of a steep external staircase similar to the neighboring homes, the stairs have been internalized and upon entry you would still ascend to the important level above the street.

Alexander Smets House.

Directly west of Smets' house on Jones Street is another house attributed to Norris. The Noah Knapp house at 10 West Jones has a slenderer street face than the previous building but has more attention paid to detail with the triangular pediments above the windows and the columns on the front porch.

Noah Knapp House.

Beside the Noah Knapp house sits a pair of double houses designed for Morris Sternberg by Alfred Eichberg in 1891. Notice that, although the detailing and fenestration on this Victorian project is dealt with in a markedly different way from the Greek Revival homes flanking it, the doors are still placed to the side, indicating a side hall plan with rooms lined up on the side of the hall.

Continue down Jones Street, crossing Whitaker, and proceeding to Barnard Street. Along the way, you will pass several more townhouses with the same side hall plan. When you come to the corner of Jones and Barnard, turn right and you will see Pulaski Square. As you walk towards the square, notice again how the larger townhouses are still turning their backs to the lane and have carriage house dependencies behind them.

Double houses built for Morris Sternberg.

Stop on Charlton Street before entering Pulaski Square and turn to the right to see two notable buildings from the early twentieth century. At 117 West Charlton there is a red brick building built for George Walker in 1904. In the southeast trust lot you will see the Jewish Educational Alliance built a decade later in 1914.

Jewish Educational Alliance, now occupied by the Savannah College of Art and Design.

Continue north on Barnard Street, leaving Pulaski Square, and stop at Liberty Street to observe the Stephen Williams house at 128 West Liberty. Although there is a hint of Greek Revival, which would have been more fashionable in 1835 when this was built, the house you are looking at might best be described as late Federal. Notice the elliptical fanlight extending past the door to rest on top of the sidelights. If you are able to stand far enough from the structure, you will notice there are two hipped roofs suggesting that the back of the house is a later addition.

Continue north to Orleans Square and, when standing by the fountain in the middle of the square, notice that over half of the houses that should surround this square are missing. Most were demolished in the early 1900s for various modern buildings. On the west side of the square there are half walls to indicate where buildings should be contributing to the street wall. Behind these walls a surface parking lot serves the civic center in the distance.

Stephen Williams House.

The Savannah Civic Center from the 1970s marks the shift from the "form follows function" mentality of the early twentieth century to the historic quoting of the later half. Although composed of a few large boxes, an arcade surrounds the Johnny Mercer Theater on the north and continues in a blind arcade around the arena on the south. The placement of glass behind sections of the arcade is reminiscent of Wallace Harrison's Metropolitan Opera House, which opened in New York in 1966. Functionally designed lighting and a concrete waffle slab canopy over the west porte-cochere add to an aesthetic current in the mid-1900s. Although heavily used, many Savannahians remember the houses sacrificed for its construction and would prefer to see the complex removed. The Civic Center has become one of the city's most threatened pieces of architecture.

Savannah Civic Center.

Back in Orleans Square, there is a small red brick building in the northwest tything lot. This deco-industrial car dealership built in 1925 still has traces of the sign reading "J.C. Lewis Motor Co" painted on the side. Notice the clerestory windows rising above the peek of the roof. These would allow natural ventilation and provide indirect lighting to the space now used by the Savannah College of Art and Design as a gallery and event venue.

J.C. Lewis Motor Co. Building, now occupied by the Savannah College of Art and Design.

The grandest house remaining on Orleans Square is the Champion-McAlpin house in the southeast trust lot. Completed in 1844 for Aaron Champion, this house was willed to the Society of the Cincinnati by Alida Harper Fowlkes in 1985. The architect attributed with the original design is Charles Blaney Cluskey. Cluskey came from Ireland to New York in 1827. It is most likely that he studied architecture in Ireland and trained with the Town and Davis firm in New York before coming to Georgia in 1829. After arriving in Savannah, Cluskey quickly moved inland to design buildings in Augusta and Milledgeville before returning to Savannah to design several houses in the 1840s.

The Champion-McAlpin house is the only attributed Cluskey house to employ the giant Tower of the Winds Order in Savannah. The Tower of the Winds is a temple in Athens documented by Stuart and Revett in their eighteenth century study of Grecian architecture. Ironically, the other building in Savannah with the same columns is the Custom House designed by John Norris. Cluskey submitted designs for the Custom House and had the backing of the local population but lost the government commission to New York architect, Norris. When Norris moved to Savannah to oversee construction, Cluskey moved to Washington, D.C.

The columns on the Champion-McAlpin house are set in antis. Ancient Greek temples occasionally extended the sidewalls past the front wall to create the porch. Columns were then placed between the sidewalls or antae, making the whole composition "in antis." The steps leading to the porch of most temples were a single straight flight spanning the width of the structure. In Savannah, William Jay started a trend in the 1820s of using the Renaissance method of splitting the stairs into double and sometimes curving steps. When attaching double curved stairs to a porch in antis, the sidewalls are implied with square pilasters in line with square columns.

Capping the Champion-McAlpin house is a mansard roof. This French Baroque form replaced the original roof in 1895 allowing the family to keep up with changing trends without having to build a new house. The cabinets, or small square rooms attached to each back corner of the house, display the original height of the building before the mansard roof was added. The rear composition of two cabinets connected by a gallery is similar to many homes in New Orleans except here the cabinets project past the sides of the house like bastions. The niches on the cabinets and the arcade under the front porch add to the eclecticism of the house by giving it a Roman touch while the geometric pattern along the bottom of the iron fence lends a bit of exotic flair. The pattern seems to be a reworking of the Greek key or meander design, named for the Meander River in present day Turkey.

Champion-McAlpin, Harper-Fowlkes House.

The same meander pattern is found along the fence of the Philbrick-Eastman house on Chippewa Square. To get to the Philbrick-Eastman house from the Champion-McAlpin house, walk along McDonough Street to the east. Both homes are attributed to Cluskey and their carriage houses would have faced each other. The second house was completed for Daniel Philbrick and Moses Eastman in 1844, the same year as the Champion-McAlpin house. Both houses have received a top floor addition, although the Philbrick-Eastman house had more alterations done to its exterior, making entrance to the building confusing. Instead of entering from the square, the front door faces McDonough Street. Originally the large curved porch facing the square was a single story high, instead of the current two-story version. In 1911, the curved porch was made the focal point of the composition with its new giant Ionic Order columns and Beaux Art ironwork. Also missing, from the current structure, are shutters, window mullions, and an arcade under the curved porch. All of these elements were designed in a similar manner to the ones on the Champion-McAlpin house.

Philbrick-Eastman House.

Although Chippewa Square is surrounded by mostly nineteenth century architecture, there are a few twentieth century buildings and a large twentieth century monument in the middle. The sculptor and architect team of Daniel Chester French and Henry Bacon completed the statue of Oglethorpe in 1910. Their most famous work is the Lincoln Memorial in Washington, D.C. On the presidential memorial, American symbols such as corn, wheat, eagles, and pinecones embellish an otherwise Greek temple. On the base of the Oglethorpe statue, there are similar garlands of pinecones, but here you will also find palmetto fronds of the low country at Oglethorpe's feet and a band of Cherokee Roses carved into the top of the marble pedestal.

Statue of James Edward Oglethorpe by Daniel French and Henry Bacon.

Before leaving Chippewa Square, you may want to stop in the recently restored space of Gallery Espresso coffee shop or see the exhibit in the lobby of the 1940s Savannah Theatre built on the foundations of William Jay's 1820 structure. Once you have finished enjoying Chippewa Square, continue south towards Madison Square.

Savannah Theatre.

While crossing Liberty Street do not miss the mansard roof on Francis Grimball's Second Empire design for Henry Brigham. Although the mansard roof was first popularized in France during the 1600s baroque era, it did not appear in the United States for almost 200 years. In the 1850s, Napoleon III took over France and created the Second Empire. Instead of using classical inspiration as his uncle Napoleon I used to link himself to Roman emperors, Napoleon III looked to the Sun King, Louis XIV and a neo-baroque style defined the Second Empire. In America, the Civil War started and construction halted in most of the country. After the conflict, Americans found the democratically inspired Greek Revival architecture less appealing, and, as with most wars, people were ready to indulge in arts that provided escapism. The first major escape during reconstruction was the idea of living in the city of romance, Paris.

Unlike the Champion-McAlpin house, the Henry Brigham house was built as a complete Second Empire structure in 1879. Notice how pilasters ending with capitals under the eave brackets define the corners. The windows on the lower levels are treated fancifully with dripstones above them not derived from classical architecture. Above the dormers, temple pediments once again cap the windows. Crowning the entire mansard roof is a frilly iron railing, or cresting, typical of the Second Empire.

Henry Brigham House.

Between Liberty Street and Madison Square is a one story Venetian Gothic armory on the west side of Bull Street. Although built for the Georgia Hussars, this building is best know to the local memory as a car dealership. The exotic quality of this small building is achieved by using two simple elements, the ogee arch and the quatrefoil motif. All of the openings are topped with an S-curved ogee arch springing from spiral columns and coming to a point with a crocket-studded pinnacle. A band of four-leaf clover shaped quatrefoils circles the top of the building.

Georgia Hussars Armory.

Across the lane is the back of another home attributed to Charles Cluskey. Go to the front of the Sorrel-Weed house to see that the fence pattern shared by the Champion and Eastman houses is continued here. While examining this bright orange home, note the primitive Doric columns and large tripartite, or three-part, windows on the parlor level. The same three section windows may be seen on the Kerr sisters' paired houses two doors to the left. Notice how the windows set into these red brick homes have a central sash with sidelights and a pediment above the entire arrangement.

Sorrel-Weed House.

Across Harris Street, you will see a John Norris structure. The home sitting in the northwest trust lot was designed for Charles Green in the Gothic Revival style. Evoking medieval castle architecture is the battlement capping the building. The same jagged crenellation can be seen on the second floor oriel windows facing Madison Square. Note the pointed gothic arches framing each pane of glass on the oriel windows and also on the cast iron fence surrounding the parterre garden. The main entry to the Green-Meldrim house is facing Saint John Episcopal Church on the south façade. Originally Macon Street ran past the door where the garden now connects the house to its current owner. The entry itself is a strong gothic element with clustered columns, crenellation, and quatrefoil.

Green-Meldrim House.

At the corner of the southwest tything lot, you will see the Scottish Rite Temple. Hyman Whitcover designed this Masonic lodge in A.L. 5913 or 1913 CE. The Masonic date can be seen, carved above the main entry, facing Bull Street. A Masonic compass is in the pediment directly above the date. The overall style of the building is neoclassical on a tripartite skyscraper form. Like a classical Roman column, the most ornamentation is at the top of this building and includes several more Masonic compasses. Look for these small blue details on shields at the corners of a scrolling band course supported by Ionic columns.

Scottish Rite Temple.

Facing the Scottish Rite Temple is the red brick Volunteer Guards Armory designed by William Gibbons Preston. This building, completed in 1892, was the first building purchased by the Savannah College of Art and Design (SCAD) in 1978 when they first opened, and it still houses the admissions department. Now know as Poetter Hall, this building is Romanesque Revival in style. Monumental Roman arches are the primary feature of the style and there are several on the lower level. Like the interior of a medieval church, two medium sized arches top some of these large arches with three smaller ones on the third floor. Castle architecture is also referenced with the corner turrets and the Bull Street entrance. The entrance is flanked by cannons attached to small turrets that rise above a battlement after being pierced with arrow loops. You may wish to step into this building to learn more about the art school or do some shopping in ShopSCAD before moving on to the next square.

Volunteer Guards Armory, the first building restored by the Savannah College of Art and Design.

Walking east from Madison Square, you will arrive in Lafayette Square. On the southwest trust lot of Lafayette Square, there is another home designed by John Norris. When this home was completed in 1849, the client was cotton merchant Andrew Low. Low's son, William, married Juliette Gordon Low and after both her father-in-law and husband were dead, Juliette lived in this house and organized the Girl Scouts. The first headquarters for the Girl Scouts is the carriage house at the back of the property. Although the Girl Scouts still own the carriage house, the Colonial Dames own and operate the main house as a museum. Notice that a two-story porch covers the back of this house. Norris's designs for Smets, Mercer, and Green all have similar rear porches, but the one on Andrew Low's house is the most exposed. Because of this, shutters now fill the openings to prevent direct afternoon sun overheating the back of the house.

Andrew Low House.

Across Charlton Street to the south of the Andrew Low house, is a home built for Low's business associate, William Battersby. The form used for Battersby's Greek Revival home is most commonly associated with Charleston. The doors facing the streets in Charleston commonly lead you onto the side porch instead of into the house. Effectively, the longer side is turned away from the street so it faces the ocean and captures the cooler breezes with more openings. Originally, the homes were a single room deep to maximize cross ventilation. This composition is the origin of the term "Charleston single house."

William Battersby House.

Diagonally across the square from Battersby's house is the Cathedral of St. John the Baptist. Designed in a refined variation of High Victorian Gothic by E. Francis Baldwin, the cathedral was built in the 1870s, after reconstruction ended. Fire destroyed the 1870s interior in 1898, and it was rebuilt with the same design. Early French Gothic architecture was Baldwin's inspiration and can be seen with the three entries framed by pointed arches. Unlike medieval French cathedrals, the doorjambs lack jamb figures and heavily carved archivolts. Directly above the center entrance is a large rose window and the outer entries are housed in the bottom of twin spire-capped towers. Attached to the slate shingled spires are elongated metal balconies. If the cathedral is open, take a moment to go in and notice the slender cast iron columns painted to look like marble. Where the nave and transept join, there are clustered columns in the same material. Recent restoration of the cathedral included the interior paint, windows, and slate on the roof.

Cathedral of St. John the Baptist.

More French influence can be found on Samuel Hamilton's house in the southeast trust lot of Lafayette Square. This home is also capped by a slate roof in a mansard form similar to the one on the Second Empire style home of Henry Brigham. The Hamilton-Turner Inn, as Hamilton's house is now known, was completed in 1872 by architect J.D. Hall. Like the Brigham house, The Hamilton-Turner Inn originally had a narrow side porch on the south façade facing Charlton Street. Unlike the Brigham home, the entry bay projects slightly from the front façade with quoins giving it more depth. The alternating rusticated blocks or quoins also define the corners of the house in a similar way to the pilasters on the Brigham house.

Walk past the back of the Hamilton-Turner Inn and cross Lincoln Street to go to Troup Square. In the stretch of Macon Street between Lincoln Street and Troup Square, notice the feel of this street is similar to the lanes that divide tything lots. With row houses in trust lots, the system of lanes is missing. In this case, the houses on both trust lots have faced out and turned their backs on each other.

Hamilton-Turner Inn.

At the end of the northwest trust lot facing Troup Square is the Unitarian Church. John Norris designed this public building in the same Gothic Revival style he used for the Charles Green house. In this case, he has included a battlement on a church design and ended up with a fortified church. Originally constructed in the 1850s on Oglethorpe Square, this brick structure was moved in the 1860s to its current location where it served for a time as an Episcopal and then a Baptist church before being purchased back by the Unitarian congregation. After the church was repurchased in the 1990s, a restoration project began with fresh stucco, replaced pinnacles, and stained glass followed by work on the interior.

Unitarian Church.

On the east side of Troup Square, the trust lot on the north was developed with a row of houses starting in 1872. The houses were designed by J.J. Dooley and built for John McDonough. Within a decade, McDonough developed the row in the south trust lot. Both rows are facing south, requiring the northern row to face their neighbors' backdoors.

Row houses built for John McDonough.

Another set of houses, built for John McDonough in 1869, sits on the northwest tything lot and currently house Firefly Café on the ground floor facing the square. This is a great place to interrupt your tour for a lunch or dinner while enjoying the view of the well-manicured square and its bronze armillary sculpture.

Double houses built for John McDonough.

The armillary that serves as Troup Square's centerpiece exhibits how the metal tradition continues into more recent times. Kenneth Lynch and Sons, of Wilton, Connecticut, created this piece in the 1970s. Another contemporary iron piece may be seen just south of Troup Square on Habersham Street. You will find the Sunflower Gate by Ivan Bailey on the right side of the street as you walk towards Jones Street. Notice how the leaves are also above the gate on the lantern and how one sunflower is turned away from the street allowing you to see its underside.

Armillary in the center of Troup Square.

On the corner of Jones and Habersham Streets, you will see two houses that are much newer than the average age for Jones Street homes. On the east side of the street is a 1970s house designed by Jerry Lominack. Although designed in a style of its time, notice the raised stoop similar to its neighbors and the similar scale being employed. Even the fenestration and materials are relatively comparable to the rest of the block. The biggest variant to the older building of the street is its manner of addressing the street wall. Most nineteenth century Savannah houses come up to the sidewalk with a flat wall and perhaps a bay window pushing out slightly. In this case, the street wall is achieved with a section of garden wall and architectural landscaping.

House designed by Jerry Lominack.

Across Habersham Street is a house designed by Daniel Snyder and completed in 2007. In this case, the contemporary home emphasizes the street wall with a solid wall and punched windows. A more open façade presents itself to the side court through a Charleston type porch.

House designed by Daniel Snyder.

Continuing south to Whitfield Square, you will pass two twentieth century buildings, the one on the left, from 1954 and on the right, from 1972. The earlier building was constructed as a nunnery. The use of primary colors became popular in the 1900s and you can see it on the nunnery with yellow bricks on the top four floors, red brick on the lower level and blue tile below three lower windows. Another grouping of three is found on the corner facing the square with three square openings placed vertically in the red brick above the cornerstone. The balconies facing Habersham Street also line up vertically and face smaller balconies on the Rose of Sharon across the street.

Marian Nunnery.

Wedding Architects of St. Petersburg, Florida, designed the large Rose of Sharon apartment building on the northwest tything of Whitfield Square. Completed in 1972, this senior housing apartment is covered with small balcony attachments. Functionally, these raw concrete attachments cannot be accessed as true balconies and serve more as awnings for the windows below them. The glazing above the main entry is shaded by a latticework of brick.

Whitfield Square is a popular location for weddings due to the gazebo in the center. Although the gazebo is from 1980, its Victorian look matches the Queen Anne houses that surround much of the square.

Although Queen Victoria reigned from 1830 until her death in 1900, lacy Queen Anne houses often come to mind when the word Victorian is mentioned. One of many styles that make up the Victorian period, the architects who developed Queen Anne homes were thinking back to medieval times and named the style for a Queen they considered appropriate to the era. The era Queen Anne reigned in is much closer to Georgian than Medieval but the name stuck.

Rose of Sharon Apartments.

The methods being used to make this new style look as though it comes from an earlier time include an asymmetrical floor plan, very active facades and lots of wood details. The overall effect is meant to feel as though the building evolved over generations. Around Whitfield Square you will see several bay windows, turrets, towers, and wrap-around porches. Before the Queen Anne style, most porches in the United States were found in the south because of the warm, humid climate creating the need for outdoor space. In the late 1800s, communication was improving and ideas were being exchanged rapidly. Commerce was also becoming more universal, and you could order sawn wood architectural components from a catalogue and have them shipped on a train to use during construction.

Double houses built for John Powers.

Notice how the new characteristics of the Queen Anne style were applied to the traditional Savannah types of double houses and row houses. On the trust lots east of the square are two variations of the double house built for John Powers. The units on the southeast were built with a common wall in 1886, but on the northeast there is a slight separation and windows on the inner walls. The separated units were completed a decade after the attached pair with John Sullivan joining John Powers in the venture. The gap between houses provides a view of the neighbor's wall but more importantly, it allows natural light into the stair hall. Inspiration for Powers and Sullivan may have come from houses going up in the southeast tything lot for Sarah Sexton, Emma Hunter, Carolina Muller, and the Home Building Company. Notice how this row of houses also uses the structural separation technique, but all units line up to create a common street wall like an attached row.

Double houses built for John Powers and John Sullivan.

As you walk down Gordon Street to the east of Whitfield Square, you will see another row on the north side of the street with Queen Anne tendencies. This time the row is attached. Stop at Price Street and take a moment to observe the houses to the east of the street. The neighborhood you are looking into is the Beach Institute Neighborhood.

Row houses built for Abraham Samuels.

The Beach Institute neighborhood bears the name of Alfred Beach, Editor of Scientific American, who donated money with the American Missionary Association for the Freedmen's Bureau to construct the institution you can still see on the corner of Price and Harris Streets. The Beach Institute was built as a school for Savannah's African Americans after the Civil War. This ethnic group was already a large part of the neighborhood that started in the 1850s as housing for railroad workers at the newly built Savannah and Albany Railroad complex.

Beach Institute, built as school by the Freedman's Bureau.

At the corner of Gordon and Price Streets there is an example of a corner store. Many of these can be found in the Beach Institute neighborhood and are easily recognized by the angled corner entrance. This simple clapboard sided structure reveals its Victorian era construction with ornamental brackets under the eaves. It was built for Casper Langlia and the Workmen and Traders Loan and Building Association in the 1880s.

Workmen and Traders Loan and Building Association, later converted to a store.

If you have time, you may want to continue down Gordon Street to East Broad or walk on another street in the Beach Institute neighborhood. You will see many examples of workers' cottages. This area has the largest concentration of cottages in the Landmark District. Although most of them were built after the Civil War, many of them could be mistaken visually for the first houses in the colony from the 1700s.

Typical cottage found in Beach Institute Neighborhood.

At the corner of Gordon and East Broad Streets, you can see Saint Francis Convent on the southwest corner. This red brick building from 1908 is now Gordon Hall for the Savannah College of Art and Design but was originally built as part of the Saint Benedict the Moor Catholic Church complex. Although the current church building, directly south of the old convent, dates from the 1950s, the parish started in 1874.

St. Benedict the Moor Catholic Church and former nunnery.

After looking at the Beach Institute neighborhood, go back through Whitfield Square to look at the Beth Eden Baptist Church facing Lincoln Street from the southwest trust lot. This High Victorian Gothic building at 302 East Gordon Street dates from 1893. Henry Urban, the architect, trained in Berlin and Paris before meeting William Gibbons Preston and going to work for him in Boston. When Preston was commissioned for the DeSoto Hotel in 1888, he appointed Urban to travel to Savannah and supervise the project. Urban made Savannah his home and completed several projects, including Beth Eden Baptist, before his death in 1927.

The design of Beth Eden Baptist illustrates why architects in England who started the High Victorian Gothic were sometimes referred to as rouge architects. Although a more modest example than some, Henry Urban intentionally employed techniques and materials not yet in existence when Gothic started. The refined red bricks that cover most of the building are also used for detailing and contrast with a band of yellow bricks at the base of the building. Along with a large, stationary stained glass rose window facing Lincoln Street, several stained glass panels are housed in operable sash windows. Rather than centering the entrance under the rose window, Urban placed it at the bottom of the splayfoot spire on the corner.

The entry to Beth Eden Baptist faces the same street as the Massie Heritage Center. If you look down Gordon Street to the west, you can see the Massie at the end of the block where the walk started in Calhoun Square. As the three main exhibits in the education facility portray, preservation is a vital part of Savannah today; the urban plan is what defines the city and determines how development occurs, but the architecture of the city is diverse and continues to reflect the population of this growing city.

Beth Eden Baptist Church.

Chapter Three
Forsyth Park

Forsyth Park marks the end of Oglethorpe's squares and the beginning of the Victorian District. Most of the buildings south of Gaston Street were built after the Civil War and some were even completed during Reconstruction, the period when the federal government tried to stabilize the country and Federal troops were stationed in southern states. In Georgia the occupation lasted until 1872.

There is plenty of free parking within a block of Forsyth Park on either the east or west side. If you park on West Hall Street, you can start your walk with the Jesse Parker Williams house, now the Savannah College of Art and Design's Smithfield Cottage.

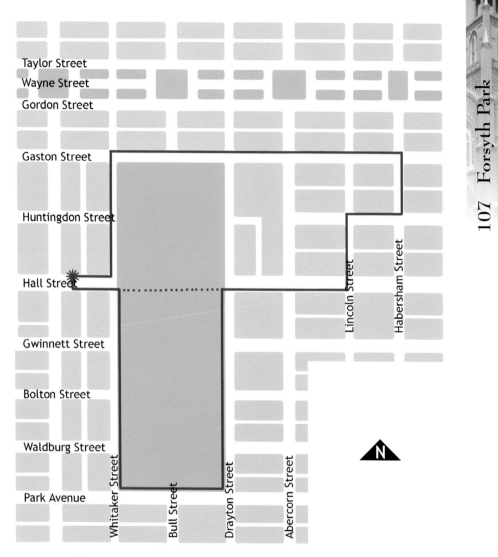

Taylor Street
Wayne Street
Gordon Street

Gaston Street

Huntingdon Street

Hall Street

Gwinnett Street

Bolton Street

Waldburg Street

Park Avenue

Whitaker Street
Bull Street
Drayton Street
Abercorn Street
Lincoln Street
Habersham Street

N

Map showing "Forsyth Park" tour with alternative extensions.

Alfred Eichberg and Calvin Fay designed Smithfield Cottage for Jesse Parker Williams in 1888. This structure at 118 West Hall Street is best categorized as Queen Anne. The active façade and wide porch are prominent characteristics of the style. Elements of particular interest on this house are the oriel window, half-timbering, and beach theme. The oriel window is the large bay window cantilevered from the house instead of supports on the ground. Notice how this example pierces the porch roof and continues to the second floor because of its use as the stairwell. Above and to the side of the oriel window are half-timbered gables. These large wood elements help give the home its intended romantic look and are further aided by the seashells dotting the stucco between.

Jesse Williams House known as Smithfield Cottage.

Between Smithfield Cottage and Forsyth Park, you will see the 1890s house now used as the Forsyth Park Inn. The inn uses a side hall plan on a corner lot. By placing the entrance on Hall Street, a side porch could be employed on the Whitaker Street façade facing Forsyth Park. This device maximized the placement on a prominent green space. This house is also a good representation of the transition from the Queen Anne style to Colonial Revival. The medieval influences of the Queen Anne style can be seen with an asymmetrical footprint, shingled bay window, and the turned spindles of the porch railing. The classical ionic columns, garland ornamentation at the top of the porch, and rectangular brackets under the eaves all show the beginnings of a Colonial Revival that would remain in the country several more decades.

Forsyth Park Inn.

On the next corner north of the Forsyth Park Inn is an example of Neoclassical, a style that closely relates to Colonial Revival. Architect Gottfried Norman built the Laurence McNeil House on the corner of Huntingdon and Whitaker Streets in 1903. The dominant feature on the McNeil House is the large curved porch with giant Corinthian Order columns. The cresting above the cornice is detailed in an alternating size anthemion pattern representing honeysuckle flowers. The whole composition of Corinthian column, entablature, and antefixa of anthemion applied to a curved porch shows a desire to emulate ancient architecture by closely resembling Roman buildings such as the Temple of Vesta and Greek structures like the Monument of Lysicrates. Norman's design becomes more playful behind the monumental porch. Note the iron balconies, Roman arched entry, and Baroque cartouche with the initials L, M, and N entwined.

Laurence McNeil House.

Whitaker Street is lined with many houses facing Forsyth Park, however it meets Gaston Street with a civic building rather than a home. Detlef Lienau designed Hodgson Hall for the Georgia Historical Society in the 1870s. Best known for bringing the Mansard roof form to America, Lienau was one of the founding members of the American Institute of Architects. After studying in Germany and Paris, this Danish architect moved to New York in 1848 and designed many fanciful Victorian buildings. By the later part of his career, he executed more rational designs with a bit of picturesque detailing added. The Georgia Historical Society fits into the later category. Without studying the building closely, the archival library could be placed into the Greek Revival style. Tuscan columns, segmental arched windows set into blind arcades, and anthemion-capped circular dormers help place the library as a more eclectic Neoclassical structure.

Georgia Historical Society's Hodgson Hall.

Diagonally across Gaston and Whitaker Streets from Hodgson Hall are two homes built just before the Civil War. Both the George Gray and William Brantley houses are tall, slender structures. The projecting front bay on the parlor level of the George Gray home to the left is a later addition. Notice how the arches from the William Brantley house on the right have been copied and embellished to form a loosely Palladian window on the Gray house. The Brantley house, completed by John Norris in 1857, uses the common technique of scoring stucco to give it the appearance of stone block construction. Less common is the cornice detail of brackets attached to an implied arcade made with stucco.

George Gray House and William Brantley House.

To the right of the William Brantley house is the last grand house built downtown, finished in 1919. George Ferguson Armstrong and his wife, Lucy Camp Armstrong, commissioned Henrik Wallin to design their home. The Beaux Arts School in Paris was influencing much of America's architecture in the early 1900s resulting in many symmetrical, white buildings with classical detailing. An Italian Renaissance influence is also apparent in features like the ceramic tiled roof, the balustrade encircled roof terrace, and the colonnaded arm curving from the front façade to screen the view of the lane. Another style used by Wallin for public buildings is the Prairie School. Although the Armstrong house does not have the traits most commonly associated with Prairie such as large overhangs, stained glass, and wood details, the midwestern influence is present on the geometric chimneys and elongated bricks. The entire composition maintains horizontality compatible with both Mediterranean inspired architecture and the Prairie style.

Armstrong House.

Across Bull Street from the Armstrong house, you will see a home built just before the Civil War as the British Consulate. The location of Edmund Molyneaux's house seems odd when you consider the main reason for a British consul's presence in Savannah was the cotton trade. Cotton was leaving from the other end of town when this structure was completed in 1857, but Forsyth Park was developed in 1853, and the neighborhood was becoming a fashionable section of Savannah. Note the use of Greek Revival, a popular American style, on the British politician's residence. The Greek Revival elements on this L-shaped townhouse include straight lines around the openings, a heavy Doric frieze containing attic windows, and a large pediment facing the lane. Originally the house had stucco, shutters, six over six panes of glass in the windows, and a two-story bay window facing Gaston Street.

Edmund Molyneaux House, now the Oglethorpe Club.

Another house with a bay window facing Gaston is the Mills B. Lane house on the corner of Drayton. This red brick, Colonial Revival home is heavily influenced by Federal period architecture. Designed by Mowbray and Uffinger in the early 1900s, many details were derived from Thomas Jefferson's work in the late 1700s. Red brick walls accented with white trim, including columned portico, are taken directly from Jeffersonian architecture. Using marble for details such as the keystone lintels, quoins, and stairs is more common in twentieth century revivalist architecture than in the original. The elliptical fanlight drawn out on the corners to cover sidelights with a large window above the entrance is common for the Federal period. Composing a one-story front porch of columns in antis under a scrolling pediment is a revivalist feature. A large middle window in a three-part composition above the entrance is common for eighteenth century homes but designing it into a bay window composition adds eclecticism to the house from the early 1900s.

Mills B. Lane House.

Across Drayton Street from the Mills B. Lane house is the Mary Lane house from 1927. The Mary Lane house is a copy of the James Habersham Jr. house discussed at the beginning of the first walk. As a recreation of an eighteenth century home, later additions to the Habersham residence were not carried over except for the Greek Revival porch added to the current Pink House restaurant after the War of 1812.

Mary Lane House.

Next to the Mary Lane house is a row built by Joseph John Dale and David Wells in the 1880s. Pattern book details such as segmental dripstones above the windows and carved wooden brackets under the eaves mark the row as Italianate. Visual depth and rhythm is added to the row with bay windows extending from ground to top story alternating with single story entry porches.

Row houses built for Joseph Dale and David Wells.

At the other end of the J. J. Dale row is a typical Italianate town-house with a large porch attached to the front. Italianate details like the segmental arches on the William Wade house at 120 East Gaston Street fade into the background behind a Renaissance Revival porch extending past the façade of the house. Symmetrical stairs invite you up from both directions and directly below the stair's landing is a lion head plaque. A balustrade lines the porch, while slender ionic columns support a second balustrade above, and the view from the porch includes a parterre garden planted in the street yard below.

William Wade House.

On the corner of Gaston and Abercorn Streets you will see another symmetrical double stair made of granite. The material has given this home its name for many years and the house built for Fred Hull is currently the Savannah College of Art and Design's Granite Hall. Restored by Jim Williams and used later as a bed and breakfast, this 1882 residence continues a symmetrical theme with full height bay windows flanking the arched entry. Roman arches on the main level, segmental arches on the top floor, bracketed eaves, and engaged columns all add to the grand quality of this Italianate structure.

Fred Hull House known as the Granite Steps.

Across Gaston Street from Granite Hall is one of Savannah's few Brutalism buildings. In stark contrast to the nineteenth century homes facing it, the raw concrete on Candler Hospital's former office area and boiler room places it firmly into the twentieth century. First popularized in France by Le Corbusier, it did not take long for the rest of the Western world to pick up the trend of using concrete in its raw state to show honesty of materials. Critics used the term "Brutalism" to describe both the hard, cold feel of the material and the forms it was molded into. On this Candler Hospital building, a regular rhythm of vertical projections gives the top portion of the building a heavy feel, aided by the solid slabs overhanging more delicate brick and small glass windows.

Candler Hospital Office Area and Boiler Room, currently used for parking.

Across Abercorn Street from Granite Hall is a project built for Algernon Hartridge in 1868 during the Reconstruction period. Although mostly composed of simple Greek Revival and Georgian elements, these homes aspire to a more fantasy based style fashionable at the time. A pointed arch, Gothic Revival arcade is applied to the top portion of the street facing façades, adding visual weight to the cornice in a unique manner.

Algernon Hartridge Houses.

At 208-210 East Gaston Street there is a pair of double houses designed by Alfred Eichberg. Notice the asymmetry being employed in this design with one monumental arched window located on the far right, balanced by a rounded bay on the far left. These homes, built for Abraham Smith and Herman Traub, exhibit a more common material for Eichberg than the clapboard and half timbering found on the Smithfield Cottage. Most of the buildings in Savannah designed by Eichberg are executed in a combination of brick and terracotta. On the Smith & Traub double houses, notice terracotta details like the dolphin plaques at the base of the monumental arched window and the capitals in rhythm with the entry arches that have sea creature faces in the middle of them. Detail continues further up the building and includes ball-shaped pressed brick placed on a diagonal circling the rounded bay.

Double houses built for Abraham Smith and Herman Traub.

More eclectic Victorian detailing can be found across Gaston Street from the Eichberg design on a set of double houses built in 1876 for Samuel Palmer and Henry Dresser. Of all the romantic revival styles drawn on, Italianate is the most dominant. It is seen on the arched windows of the lower level and brackets under the eaves. The arches from the windows are echoed in the porch structures, but the spandrels are filled with quatrefoils cut from wood. These Carpenter Gothic details are joined by Greek Revival pediments above the upper storey windows.

Double houses built for Samuel Palmer and Henry Dresser.

Continue another block and a half to see another double house composition common to this neighborhood. One of several houses built for grocer John Entelman, this pair from 1892 has matching domes. Gingerbread scrollwork and spindles on the front porch connecting the polygonal bays that support the domes place an otherwise boxy structure into the Queen Anne style. Although the ribbed domes add some exotic flair to the double houses, the form is taken from the octagonal Renaissance precedent set with the Florence Cathedral.

Double houses built for John Entelman.

More exotic domes than the ones on Entelman's double houses are found further south on a pair built for the McMillan brothers at 511-513 Habersham Street. Completed in 1895, this pair has brackets and segmental arches from the Italianate, but executed in a simpler manner than earlier in the century. Like the Entelman houses across the street, this pair has bays connected by a Queen Anne porch. Capping the polygonal bays, this set of domes achieves a more exotic quality by using an ogee profile, being concave on the lower portion with a convex portion placed at the top.

Double houses built for the McMillan Brothers.

Like many landowners in this neighborhood, the McMillan brothers built several projects similar to each other including a pair facing Huntingdon Street directly south of the pair at 511-513 Habersham Street. In 1892, three years before both of these projects were completed, they finished a row with a different look across Habersham Street. The most outstanding feature of 402-410 East Huntingdon Street is its use of polychromy or multicolored brickwork emulating High Victorian Gothic architecture from earlier in the century in England. The true Gothic influence is seen in the front porch accented with Tudor arches, pointed trefoil arches, and quatrefoils along the width of the row. Elements from Italianate and Romanesque Revival are also found within the design but the massing of the entire project pushes it towards the Queen Anne style. With this project, the McMillan bothers achieved an extremely eclectic, Victorian mix.

After studying the five-unit McMillan row from the front, turn left and walk down Huntingdon Street to the west. At the corner of Huntingdon and Lincoln Streets you will find another set of McMillan double houses. This pair, from 1888, has a set of domes similar to the first set. In this case, the structure is covered in stucco but still employs a mixture of Queen Anne, Italianate, Gothic, Romanesque, and Renaissance revivals.

Row houses built for the McMillan Brothers.

Across Lincoln Street is a large red brick structure designed by Alfred Eichberg. As you study this 1890 mass more closely, you will notice it is another double house—this time built for brothers, George and Irwin Tiedeman. Although an eclectic mix, the Tiedeman house is strongly characteristic of the Romanesque Revival popularized by H.H. Richardson. Notice the use of brick and terracotta similar to Eichberg's design for the Smith-Traub double house. The monumental arching is also employed and accented by rough-hewn stone. An active façade is achieved with patterns, massing, and materials.

Double houses built for the Tiedeman Brothers.

William Gibbons Preston designed a similar structure to the Tie-deman double house for George and Lucy Baldwin. Proceed south on Lincoln Street until you come to Hall Street to find this 1888 building. Both George Tiedeman and George Baldwin were important Savan-nahians. Among other things, Tiedeman was mayor of Savannah and Baldwin served on the Cotton Exchange Board that hired Preston to come to Savannah and design their building. Both houses and the Cotton Exchange were built with red brick and terracotta details. The Richardsonian Romanesque home built for Baldwin also employs an asymmetrical floor plan and multi-leveled entrance stair.

The same year Preston's design was completed for the Baldwins, American architect, Frank Lloyd Wright, who would later become well known, started training under his mentor, Louis Sullivan. Sullivan hired Wright in 1888 at a time when Queen Anne and other Victorian styles such as Romanesque Revival were most common in this country. Although Wright's influences were many and varied, the techniques his early Prairie houses are best known for can be seen in homes like the Baldwin house with its meandering entry stair, open plan interior, and geometric ironwork. The ironwork on the stair is still more curvilinear than Wright would design but the railing above the porch is pushing further into the Arts-and-Crafts movement. Even more geometric iron is found directly to the west of the Baldwin house with a porch attached to an Italianate home built for Dr. Julius LeHardy.

George and Lucy Baldwin House.

Before continuing down Hall Street, you will see a Kroger supermarket on the far side of its parking lot. The front façade of this 1990s building is designed to resemble the north and south façades of the 1880s City Market structure demolished in the 1950s. The removal of the Victorian market designed by Augustus Schwaab ignited an awareness of threats to historic buildings. Shortly after it was torn down, Historic Savannah Foundation formed. Nostalgia for the lost building can be seen in this Kroger façade, a picture of the older building just inside the entrance of the newer one, and the park that replaced a parking garage on the site of the former City Market.

Kroger supermarket copied after the old City Market.

Continue down Hall Street, crossing Abercorn Street, and going all the way back to Forsyth Park to find another picturesque house similar to the Tiedeman and Baldwin houses. At the corner of Hall and Drayton Street is the Mansion on Forsyth Park. Started as a single-family home for Lewis Kayton in 1889, most of this complex is 2000s construction for a five-star hotel. Alfred Eichberg designed the original mansion, now operated as the hotel's restaurant, in the Romanesque Revival style with many Flemish inspired details. The most obvious element coming from the Flemish or Dutch culture is the curved gable

repeated around the top of the building. The Romanesque influence is present with monumental arches that were adopted in the new construction and lead to the lobby entry. Above the main entrance, another Flemish gable quotes the older construction. Medieval inspired towers bookend the Drayton Street façades facing Forsyth Park.

You may choose to end your tour here since you are back in Forsyth Park. If you have not explored the south end of the park, you might enjoy a continued journey around this former militia parade ground.

Lewis Kayton House, now restaurant for the Mansion on Forsyth Park.

Forsyth Park was developed in the 1850s as Forsyth Place. City planners in industrializing nations were talking about the need for green spaces to relieve the tedium of polluted cities. Although Savannah already contained an abundance of green spaces, it responded

to the urban planning trends and hired landscape gardener, Wilhelm Bischoff, to install the northern end of the current park. The centerpiece at this end of the park comes from New York where a foundry was making copies of a popular fountain in Paris.

Fountain anchoring north end of Forsyth Park.

After the Civil War in the 1860s, Forsyth was extended to include militia parade grounds at the south end. The military use continued in the early 1900s when white follies that you can still see in the park were constructed as dummy forts used for drilling during World War I. The centerpiece at this end of the park is the Confederate Monument sculpted in Canada by Robert Reid.

South end of Forsyth Park comprised of forts, monument, and parade grounds.

Surrounding the south end of Forsyth Park are nineteenth and twentieth century houses, offices, and institutional buildings. Walking south on Drayton Street from the Mansion on Forsyth Park, you will come upon an office building now used by the Red Cross at 906 Drayton Street. Notice how the façade facing Forsyth Park is composed of a glass wall set back into a protruding frame. The entrance is called out with a vertical plane that extends both out and up from the building and supports a smaller horizontal plane used as the awning to the entry. Dating from the 1950s, this two-story structure was designed in a style coming from the Bauhaus.

The Bauhaus started as a school in Germany in the early 1900s as a reaction to the romantic revivalist architecture it followed. While styles from the Victorian era were partially formed as a nostalgic reaction to the Industrial Revolution, they came to represent architecture only for the elite. One of the aims of the Bauhaus and other contemporary movements was to make architecture more accessible. Health issues were also a concern as multiple families crowded into run down mansions and tenements. Design coming from the Bauhaus emphasized an interaction of spaces, materials, and clean lines, rather than applied ornamentation. As Germany's political landscape altered in the lead up to World War II, many designers from the Bauhaus moved to the United States. American architecture schools quickly adopted them, and the influence can be seen across the country.

Office building now occupied by the American Red Cross.

Continue walking to the south end of Forsyth Park to see two institutional buildings across Park Avenue. Between Drayton and Bull Streets, the former Telfair Hospital is on the left, and the Chatham Artillery Armory complex is on the right. Designed by Alfred Eichberg and Calvin Fay, the Telfair Hospital dates from 1886. The building is now the Telfair Arms Apartments, but the hospital organization still exists as the longest running women's hospital in the country and operates through the Candler Hospital originally located at the opposite end of the park. Although the physical location of the health organization is now in a newer neighborhood, this building represents a philanthropic desire to help the ill and poor at the end of the 1800s.

Telfair Arms Hospital now used as senior housing.

The building that shares this block with the Telfair Hospital was constructed as the Chatham Artillery Armory. Flanking the main entrance on Bull Street are shields with the dates 1789 and 1913, the year the artillery formed and the year of the current structure. Now used by the American Legion with shops and restaurants in the lower side wings, the National Guard occupied this building when the Eighth Air Force was activated in it in 1942. Note the use of Neo-Gothic for the armory design.

Chatham Artillery Armory.

You will find three more twentieth century buildings on the west side of the park. Continue along Park Avenue to Whitaker Street and look across the street to see them. The first two are office buildings with low profiles and clean lines. Although both buildings are clad with brick, notice the yellow brick on the one to the left. The brick is arranged in a stack bond and by not overlapping, reveals itself as a veneer and not structural brick. It also creates a more uniform wall and gives the entrance more importance. Exposed concrete frames the entry and steps in twice on either side, giving more importance to the deco relief above the glass.

Twentieth century building with yellow brick laid in stack bond.

The building to the right has brick arranged in a stretcher bond, but the ribbon window band above the brick reveals that the brick is not supporting the roof. Instead of a load-bearing wall, internal columns support the roof. The composition of the roof is a waffle slab that extends past the wall to form an overhanging eave. Like the building to the left, the doors are glass panels with fixed glass panels to the sides. The entry is emphasized with three arches made of metal and glass.

Twentieth century building with ribbon window under eaves.

Three arches also emphasize the front of the George Walker house next door. Built in 1911, the home at 911 Whitaker Street is in an Italian Renaissance Revival style designed by Hyman Witcover. Although the same architect of the ornate City Hall and Scottish Rite Temple, Witcover is more restrained on this residential project. A few choice elements reveal the Renaissance influence such as the balusters leading up the staircase, paired brackets supporting the overhanging eave, garland on the columns of the second story porch, and oval dormers which echo the first floor arches from the roofline.

Continue north on Whitaker Street passing several homes from the late 1800s to get back to Hall Street where the tour started with the Smithfield Cottage. The Forsyth Park Inn marks the corner of Hall and Whitaker Streets and lines up with the seam separating the original portion of the park from its extension. Today the diverse nature of Savannah's architecture is reflected in the many uses of Forsyth Park. You may be lucky enough to be in the park during a jazz concert or Shakespeare performance. In the spring, students and alumni give a free art show when the Savannah College of Art and Design hosts the Sidewalk Arts Festival. Dog lovers bring their furry friends out for the Mutt Strut and social planners relish a picnic competition. A wedding may be using the fountain as a backdrop while intramural sports teams practice lacrosse, soccer or frisbee on the south end and, on occasion, a group of soldiers will still leave their local base to come drill in the old parade grounds.

George Walker House.

Bibliography

Avery, Carlos P. *E. Francis Baldwin: The B&O, Baltimore, and Beyond.* Baltimore, Maryland: Baltimore Architecture Foundation, 2003.

Cox, James A.D. and N. Jane Iseley. *Savannah Tour of Homes and Gardens.* Savannah, Georgia: Christ Church & Historic Savannah Foundation, 1996.

Curl, James Stevens. *Dictionary of Architecture.* Oxford, England: Oxford University Press, 1999.

D'Alonzo, Mary Beth. *Streetcars of Chatham County: Photographs from the Collection of the Georgia Historical Society.* Charleston, South Carolina: Arcadia Publishing, 1999.

Elmore, Charles J. Ph.D. *Savannah Georgia.* Charleston, South Carolina: Arcadia Publishing, 2002.

Follett-Thompson, Jean Ames. *William Gibbons Preston and architectural professionalism in Boston During the second half of the nineteenth century.* Thesis: Boston University, 1986.

Frey, Valerie and Kaye Kole. *The Jewish Community of Savannah.* South Carolina: Arcadia Publishing, 2002.

Gunther, Justin. *Historic Signs of Savannah: Photographs from the Collection of the Georgia Historical Society.* Charleston, South Carolina: Arcadia Publishing, 2004.

Johnson, Charles J. Jr. *Mary Telfair: The Life and Legacy of a Nineteenth-Century Woman.* Savannah, Georgia: Frederic C. Beil, 2002.

Jones, Carmie M., ed. *Historic Savannah: A Survey of Significant Buildings in the Historic Districts of Savannah, Georgia, 3rd ed.* Savannah, Georgia: Historic Savannah Foundation, 2005.

Kelley, David E. *Building Savannah*. Charleston, South Carolina: Arcadia Publishing, 2000.

Kingery, Dr. Dorothy Williams. *More Than Mercer House: Savannah's Jim Williams & His Southern Houses*. Savannah, Georgia: Sheldon Group L.L.C., 1999.

Kramer, Ellen Weill. *The Domestic Architecture of Detlef Lienau, a Conservative Victorian*. West Conshohocken, Pennsylvania: Infinity Publishing, 1961/2006.

Lane, Mills. *Savannah Revisited: History & Architecture, 5th ed.* Savannah: Beehive Press, 1969/2001.

Lerski, Hanna Hryniewiecka. *William Jay: Itinerant English Architect 1792-1837*. Lanham, Maryland: University Press of America, 1983.

McAlester, Virginia and Lee. *A Field Guide to American Houses*. New York, New York: Alfred A. Knopf, 1984/2002.

Middleton, R. and D. Watkin. *History of World Architecture: Architecture of the Nineteenth Century*. Milan, Italy: Electa Architecture, 2003.

Morrison, Mary Lane. *John S. Norris, Architect in Savannah, 1846-1860*. Savannah, Georgia: Beehive Press, 1980.

Morrison, Mary Lane, ed. *Historic Savannah, 2nd ed.* Savannah, Georgia: Historic Savannah Foundation, 1979.

Pinkerton, Connie Capozzola, Maureen Burke, Ph.D., and the Historic Preservation Department of the Savannah College of Art and Design. *The Savannah College of Art and Design: Restoration of An Architectural Heritage*. Charleston, South Carolina: Arcadia Publishing, 2004.

Poppeliers, John C. and S. Allen Chambers. *What Style is it?: A Guide to American Architecture*. New York, New York: John Wiley & Sons, Inc., 2003.

Reps, John W. *The Making of Urban America: A History of City Planning in the United States*. Princeton, New Jersey: Princeton University Press, 1965.

Safdie, Moshe. *Beyond Habitat*. Cambridge, Massachusetts: The M.I.T. Press, 1970/1973.

Spracher, Luciana M. *Lost Savannah: Photographs from the Collection of the Georgia Historical Society*. Charleston, South Carolina: Arcadia Publishing, 2002.

Staurt, James and Nicholas Revett. *The Antiquities of Athens and Other Monuments in Greece*. London, England: Elibron Classics, 1837/2005.

Sully, Susan. *Savannah Style: Mystery and Manners*. New York, New York: Rizzoli, 2001.

Toledano, Roulhac. *The National Trust Guide to Savannah: Architectural & Cultural Treasures*. New York, New York: John Wiley & Sons, Inc., 1997.